# SAFARI

EXPERIENCING THE WILD

Photographs and Notes by Neil Leifer

# S A F

## EXPERIENCIN

# A   R   I

Essay by Lance Morrow

## G   T H E   W I L D

The Reader's Digest Association, Inc.    Pleasantville, N.Y./Montreal

Designed by  Tom Bentkowski
          Tom Vincent

A Reader's Digest Book

Library of Congress
Cataloging in
Publication Data

Leifer, Neil.
      Safari : experiencing the wild / photographs and notes by Neil Leifer ;
          text by Lance Morrow.
            p.   cm.
      ISBN 0-89577-458-5
      1. Zoology—Africa—Popular works.   I. Morrow, Lance.   II. Title.
QL336.L45   1992
599.096—dc20                                              92-25587

READER'S DIGEST and the Pegasus logo are registered trademarks of
The Reader's Digest Association, Inc.

Printed in the United States of America

For Jodi and Corey, two very special kids

**W**e flew all night across the breadth of Africa, the vast blank below, and just after dawn we dropped into Nairobi like a meteorite.

I was dazed and travel-weary, 23 hours from New York. I checked into the Norfolk Hotel and slid into a shallow, surreal sleep, then woke to bright afternoon sunshine and the songs of African birds in the aviary of the Norfolk courtyard, and to the soft, low music of Swahili being spoken below my window. I tried to remember the dream I had just dreamed, but I could not.

Neil Leifer had come to Kenya to photograph the animals. I had come merely to look at them. In order to give the looking another possible layer of meaning, I carried along the idea of asking people in Africa what kind of dreams they had about the wild animals.

The city-dwelling American high-rise child dreams about wild things, about lions and so on. My five-year-old son, Justin, has nightmares about animals he has never seen. There are beasts wandering around in the subconscious of people who spend their days amid concrete and steel and glass. What does an African boy who lives among the animals—a Masai, for example—dream about? Are the dreams the same? My impulse was not clinical—certainly not Freudian, but if anything, Jungian in some vague way. The animals of Africa are powerfully original forms—the art naif of a collective unconscious, I supposed. I wanted to see what becomes of the animals in the minds of people among whom the beasts' presence is not unconscious memory but daily fact.

In the weeks that followed I would collect dreams from Masai and Kikuyu schoolchildren, from schoolteachers, from witch doctors, from Masai warriors and safari guides, from white ranchers and game catchers and naturalists. And from myself. It was a way of seeing the animals.

In order to meet Neil, I hitched a ride with another American photographer, Bill Campbell, driving north from Nairobi in his Land Rover toward Mt. Kenya. The press of population is evident everywhere in Nairobi, of course, and in the countryside beyond, the land broken up into *shambas,* small farms as densely packed, side by side, as the geometric paddy fields that you see from the bullet train on the ride between Tokyo and Osaka: every square meter of useful land occupied. Kenya has the world's highest rate of population growth—4 percent annually—and half the population is under the age of 15. I wondered where the animals could live.

The old asphalt roads from British colonial days were crumbling. They looked as if a large, tar-eating animal had been chewing at them from the shoulders, inward toward the center line. Driving on them can be a harrowing experience. The vehicle speeds down the dead center of the road like a rhino charging, and only at the last instant the driver flicks a wrist to the left (British rules: drive on the left). All morning we were passed by the taxis called matatus, which hurtle along with three or four times as many passengers as they were intended to hold, arms or whole bodies hanging out the windows. The matatu was the wildest creature that I saw until we reached Nanyuki and pulled onto the private game preserve of the Mount Kenya Safari Club.

There we rattled across a cattle guard, almost in the shadow of Mount Kenya, left the Third World, with its tattered and teeming human life, and entered a different dimension almost—a primal garden, or the illusion of one. Here I passed from messy history into what Shiva Naipaul called "the primal heraldic world of Karen Blixen and her friends." Here I found giraffes and zebras grazing in long grasses, not far from the road, and oblivious to us as we passed. I felt as if we had become invisible, sliding like ghosts through this abrupt beauty under a golden late-afternoon sun that glinted off the hides and spiraling horns, and off the snaggletoothed snow temples of Mount Kenya above us.

The Mount Kenya Safari Club looks like a Westchester County country club set down in East Africa, decorated with lion skins and trophy tusks from the old days (pre-1976), when hunting was legal. Peacocks yowl like cats around the grounds, and prehistoric birds goose-step across the golfing green with a proprietary air.

Neil had already arrived, and we had dinner that night with Alan Binks, who would be our safari guide. Binks is a sharp-eyed, urbane Englishman who came out to Kenya as an adolescent, became a citizen and settled there. Alan is himself a nature photographer of some accomplishment. As safari guide, he managed effortlessly to merge the roles of white hunter, naturalist, hotel manager, straw boss, chauffeur, raconteur, diplomat, and drinking companion.

Waking next morning, I looked out the window to see astonishing laminations of light—first the dawn sun on grasses, pond and trees, and then above them in the middle distance, a layer of dark gray-blue mist topped by successive layers of mist and light, a vertical spectrum from dark to white, and higher still, in the splendid distance and absolutely clear air, Mount Kenya's uncut crystal peaks.

We drove east on the crumbling, potholed roads through shamba country, the routes busy with market traffic and lined with roadside stands selling produce, mostly African calabashes that smelled of dense hut-smoke, and iron and copper bracelets made of wires twisted into coils, then beaten flat. In an hour the driver, Simeon Londaga, turned the Land Cruiser onto a dirt washboard road. Children beside the track waved gaily at the passing vehicles, even those that roared by and left them standing in clouds of dust. Their mothers, however—women stooped under loads of wood or other burdens—glared after us as we receded, like Mister Toad. I did not blame them. But it occurred to me that if I remonstrated with the driver and asked him to go slower as we passed pedestrians, it would throw off his travel schedule. And I would have started off our safari by telling him his business, in his own country. So I waved back at the children and we shot onward, scattering dust into the Kikuyu behind us. It only occurs to me now, in retrospect, that Simeon, as a Masai, may have held the Kikuyu in the traditional tribal contempt, and so may not have minded leaving them in dust.

y noon we came to Meru, a 700-square-mile game park, and there seriously began looking for the animals. Again, the bustling, tattered human Africa vanished behind us at the border of the animals' territory. I felt as if we had left earth's gravity, or time's gravity, and the late 20th century's urgencies, and now were sliding through some other dimension, passing across a sere plain among doum palms, like tall, lithe candelabra, and whistling thorn acacias—my favorites—flat-topped, with a sort of Japanese delicacy about them. From branches hung the globular nests of weaver birds, like pale Christmas ornaments. Here and there a gesticulating baobab, heavy and gnarled and somehow suggesting druidic powers. Off to the west above the plain, in a purple distance-haze, lay the Nyambeni Hills. The midday sun banged straight down upon us, shadowless, a whitish equatorial glare.

We met an array of 31 reticulated giraffes that stood as we approached, like alert statuary. I poked my head through the Land Cruiser's sunroof, a cushion jammed behind me to absorb the rougher jolts, and I counted the giraffes. When we seemed to move into their critical distance—their inviolable buffer of safe space between us and them—they set off in their thundering run. They left behind them an oryx, grazing solo, undisturbed.

All afternoon we bounced across the landscape, slowing sometimes to crawl in four-wheel drive across dry washes or hills knobby with black volcanic boulders. Simeon managed the Land Cruiser with a gingerly precision. It seemed to me that he accorded the car and its engine the same respectful care he gave to the animals—detached wonder mixed with a sense of professional collaboration.

Simeon's eyesight was astonishing. He clearly loved the animals. He could see them and identify them at distances when they seemed mere specks or stones to me—at distances, in fact, when I would have said the creature he pointed out was just a mote in my own eye, a sort of subjective maculation.

Once during the afternoon Simeon pointed and said in his flat, quiet English, which I always needed an instant to unravel: "Lee-oh-pard!"

I followed the line of his arm and finger and tried to make my eyes focus upon the leopard that he claimed was there in the limbs of a distant tree. But I could not. He moved the Land Cruiser closer and closer, now and then pointing: "Lee-oh-pard. He has gazelle." The leopard drags its kill up into a tree and parks it there in a fork of branches, out of reach of scavengers and lesser diners. It is an amazing feat of strength, routinely accomplished. Then over a period of days, the leopard, a loner, returns to the stash to eat.

That leopard eluded me, although I learned never to mistrust Simeon's sightings. If he said the animal was there, the animal was there: it merely took my myopic and inexperienced city eyes a few more minutes to find the creature out there in its camouflaged universe. Later when I asked, Simeon told me that the leopard is his favorite among the animals—"because it is beautiful, because of its spots."

I felt literary. Two lines of W.B. Yeats came into my head: *"Man is in love and loves what vanishes. What more is there to say?"* It was a thought that would drift through my thinking about the animals in the weeks to come. The entire expedition comes back to me now as a splendid mirage. I applied Yeats's words not only to the illusory quality of the animals in the bush but also, in a larger way, to their impermanence on the earth.

Pretty early on a trip like this, one develops a queer kind of premonitory sense of mourning about the African animals, followed soon by an angry desire to do something to protect them. But protected, as they are in the game parks, they are like a child that must live in a germ-free bubble, which is Edenic enough, but grotesquely artificial.

When Neil and I met Anna Merz, she was presiding sadly and defiantly over a handful of rhinos-in-a-bubble in Lewa Downs. Merz, a tough, direct Englishwoman with something of the rhino in her own character has lived in Africa much of her life, and has established a refuge to try to keep rhinos alive, out of the hands of poachers. She fenced in 7,500 acres of her land, where about 16 remnant rhinos were living when we came to visit her. "Poor buggers!" Anna Merz said, talking about her rhinos, her eyes flashing bright indignation. "It is a sin and a crime that animals should be driven to the brink of extinction, especially by something as idiotic as a dagger handle." In 1970 there were 20,000 rhinos in Kenya; by 1992 there were fewer than 410. Merz carried a spike-headed club under the seat of her car. She was not licensed to carry a gun, but employed guards with old Enfield rifles to patrol the refuge. But the Somali poachers travel in gangs of 50 and more, armed with automatic weapons.

For a time, early in the safari, I was almost childishly depressed by the managed relationship of the animals, the sense of game park as a kind of nostalgic diorama. Alan Binks told me one night around a campfire that his employers, the safari outfitters Ker and Downey, had once considered putting electronic darts in leopards so that they could be more easily located. "But," said Binks, "we decided that would take the fun out of it."

When Theodore Roosevelt made his great safari to East Africa in 1909, he later wrote grandiloquently: "On the land and on the water, there are dread beasts that feed on the flesh of man....The land teems with beasts of the chase, infinite in number and incredible in variety. It holds the fiercest beasts of ravin, and the fleetest and most timid of those beings that live in undying fear of talon and fang—" Part of the exhilaration for Roosevelt was his highly developed, even lurid, sense of danger. He debated with white hunters about which of the terrible beasts was the most dangerous—the lion, the Cape buffalo, the rhinoceros, the elephant when cornered or enraged. Some argued it was the rhino—massive, fast and stupid, given to charging anything on the wind. Somewhat the same for the Cape buffalo. Roosevelt's most grandiloquent respect went to the lion. He wrote of one wounded male: "He was a magnificent beast, with a black and tawny mane; in his prime, teeth and claws perfect, with mighty thews, and savage heart....His life had been one unbroken career of rapine and violence, and now the maned master of the wilderness, the terror that stalked the night, the grim lord of slaughter, was to meet his doom at the hands of the only foes who dared molest him." Roosevelt liked to think of himself as a man in elemental combat against fierce beasts of the Pleistocene. He savored the danger.

In East Africa these days one always hears stories about people "hammered" by buffaloes. Now and then a tourist does something stupid or merely unlucky and gets hurt by an animal. Sometimes there are anomalies: I know a Laikipia rancher named John Hall and his daughter, Susan, who were attacked by hyenas in the middle of the night in the remote Chalbi Desert in the northern frontier district. Hall fired a shotgun at the charging male hyenas, and father and daughter made it to their car and escaped, just barely. But that attack was a rarity, a curiosity. These days it is humankind that endangers the animals, not the other way around.

**M**ore literature: Binks told me one day about a client of his who spent all of his safari with his head buried in a book—a collection of the works of Graham Greene. While Binks (in mounting anger and mystification) went through the motions of safari, driving the roads, finding the animals, the client barely took his eyes off the pages of Greene's despondent fiction, except to lean back now and then and laugh heartily at something he had read. Binks thought this was a wonderful example of queer and unpredictable human-animal behavior. I liked the story too, but thought I detected some buried logic in the man's behavior—something to do with Greene's bleak feel for things and the purgatorial dilemma of the African wildlife, with the depressing, exigent human life crowding in and fencing the animals' ranges and shooting them down for tusks and pelts and horns.

But the road always cheered me up. Nothing that I know is more cheering than the sight of wild animals in open country. Why? Freedom is exhilarating. So is great space and distance. So are the bizarre and perfect primal forms of trees and animals. They possess the power of their own originality and their magic matter-of-factness—and above everything else, the power of their indifference to the human world, their alien's self-sufficiency, their perfect otherness.

I found that I dreamed somewhat differently in Africa—or more vividly. Later in the trip, while staying in a Masai boma in the Loita Hills, I dreamed that I raided cattle on West 57th Street in Manhattan. I loaded four stolen cows into a cattle trailer towed by an old Chrysler Imperial and drove them up across the Connecticut border. On another night, I dreamed about my two sons, playing in a northern American meadow on the edge of pine woods, the boys frisking in tall grass.

I did not dream often about the wild animals. One night I dreamed of goats being dipped and then driven wildly here and there by African herdboys. Then of a tame waterbuck that I petted, and a gorilla that asked for a cigarette. In another dream, I was walking in Bronxville, New York, with Laurence I. Barrett, the White House correspondent of *Time*. A lion approached and started tough-talking to Larry in the accents of a small-time Brooklyn gangster, and ended by extending a paw and muttering, "Gimme five!"

Our trip in actuality had a quality of waking hallucination, of bright preconsciousness. I found the animals' motions and forms to be dreamlike, a word that recurs in my notebooks.

One afternoon, I went to the Morijo Loita Primary School, a windswept arrangement of tin-roofed buildings on a bare hillside. Several dozen schoolchildren were gathered in a classroom of the sort that made me think of places where Abraham Lincoln went to school on the Indiana frontier. The children sat in rows at long, crude benches. They were asked about their encounters with wild animals, in reality and in dreams. A boy named Seketo told of being chased by a lion once while he was herding cows. He said that normally when a boy meets a wild animal, the solution is simple: the boy runs one way, the animal runs another, both are happy.

In dreams, the children were paralyzed with fright. A girl named Hyinka dreamed that when she went into the forest for firewood, a Cape buffalo attacked her and tried to push her down with his horns. She could neither run nor scream. The buffalo pushed her down into the water with his nose. Memusi had a dream about a lion's attacking and biting, and she tried to scream but could not. Lekerenka could not scream either, when bitten in his dreams by a spitting cobra. He woke up crawling on the the ground.

I conceived a modest theory about dreams. The difference between the Kenya nightmares and the scary dreams of a five-year-old boy in New York City might be that the beasts of primal fantasy live just outside the Masai huts. The Masai reside, so to speak, in the psychic forest, where the wild things are. The beasts there were not invented by an illustrator. They are the originals. The lion roars in the Masai's sleep, and roars when the Masai wakes as well.

So to some extent, the world inside the skull corresponds to the world outside it, an interesting reconciliation. The inner eye and the outer eye may sometimes see the same image, the same dreamy beast standing under the fever tree. The sleeping and the waking become interchangeable. The actual and the psychic coincide.

Beside the road in Meru a lion had killed a porcupine during the night—it must have been a messy, painful task. Simeon pointed out the evidence: the scattered quills, the lion's pug marks, the scene-of-the-accident scuffle-tracks in the dust.  Not far away now were yellow-necked spur-fowl, and much birdsong in the air, and in the middle distance, two lesser kudu nipping the beige-white grasses, and beyond them a herd of zebras in their short-shouldered abstraction. Two male zebras left off grazing and began to frisk and bite the air at each other's flanks, with tossing heads, whether fighting or merely playing I could not tell. Then they just as quickly lost the impulse and went back dreamily to their grasses.

A crested eagle flapped screaming off the top of a doum palm tree and then rose and rose in the faultless sky, and at last rode the thermals, searching the landscape with eyes that were even better than Simeon's.

Under a fig tree, a crowd of baboons socialized—grooming one another, darting from group to group in their busy agenda. A baby, backing up, tumbled in a backflip across a small log, and then stared in astonishment at his mother, as if she had done the mischief. The mother kept on obliviously at her gossip with two other females. But when our car drew closer, all the baboons, as if on a common signal, accomplished a kind of darting evaporation into the leaves and trees, and soon we saw eyes and faces peering out at us, questioning.

Sand crows in the dust on the road, lovely little birds.  Then, not far off, the skull of a Cape buffalo killed by a lion, a week ago, says Simeon. In a declivity of the road by a small river, a male waterbuck with ten wives. He saw us, and he ushered the females irritably across the road, snorting and dancing a little, enforcing discipline against danger. The waterbuck would become, for some reason, a favorite of mine. I liked its amiable size, bigger than the gazelle, less delicate, less fleet and neurotically alert, but graceful all the same, in a bouncy way.

We wandered, searching among the animals all afternoon. Here was a solo ostrich endlessly switching its wings like feather dusters, alternating as it made its clumsy and fastidious way through grasses by the slummy condominium of a termite mound.

We anthropomorphize the animals, assign to them the shades of human character and mood and virtue and vice and even social class. We see royalty and nobility among them, and peasant classes and petit bourgeois, see tragedy and farce—the variations of human behavior projected back onto Pleistocene creatures. The elephant in its grandeur belongs to the highest royalty. The lion has kingly moments, but I came to see it sometimes as the Masai herders often do—as a big, dangerous pest. The Cape buffalo: massive, dark, awesome brooder, full of power, somehow shaggily Slavic, an Eisenstein medieval Muscovite beast. Or the rhinoceros: dangerous in the wild, but now so beleaguered as to be more pathetic than menacing—an armor-plated orphan, the prehistoric Anastasia of creatures, last of the Romanovs.

The leopard: in Swahili, they say he is *kali*. That means fierce, or something more than fierce—fierce on the African scale of fierceness, which is impressive. I saw only three leopards on our safari. I heard one roar-growling once, a conscienceless, terrifying noise, like a satanic chain saw on slow idle. I don't assign much social class to the leopard—or if I did: a beautiful sinister aristocrat, perhaps. We had some games learning Swahili. *Wapi chou* means, "Where is the toilet?" *Wapi chui* means, "Where is the leopard?" Both are important questions, but it would be dangerous and ludicrous to get the answers confused.

The warthog became a source of great pleasure. He is a briskly unattractive character, but has a superbly strutty and confident gait—a bucky trot. When he runs, he holds his piggy tail straight up in the air like a flag. Simeon said the tail is a figure "1." "I'm Number One," Simeon imitated, grinning. The warthog can be dangerous. He lives in holes dug by hyenas or ant bears, and when cornered there, he comes firing out of the hole like a cannonball. And he uses his tusks like a razor in a bar fight.

What of the clerical and dowager class of bird? The kori bustard looks like a vulture ascended into the respectable middle classes. The secretary bird, aptly named, is a splendid priss on stilts.

We almost never saw snakes—*Nyoka!* I had an impression that the Africans never mentioned them to us, perhaps on instructions. They were there all right, but fortunately mostly shy, and quick enough to vanish well before human arrival. In any case, we were watching animals mostly from the safety of our vehicles.

**B**ut then one day many months later, on a different trip to Africa, I was on foot, walking through the Mathews Range in the Northern Frontier District with friends. We were straggling into camp one evening, our noisy animal-scattering procession including ten Samburu men, ten donkeys, and a mule. Lutupin, a young Samburu who led the march, heard a noise in the grass beside the little river and grinned: *"Nyoka!"* Lutupin was afraid of nothing. I turned in time to see a cobra as thick as a New York City fire hose sliding slowly away through the grass.

East Africa is endlessly theatrical. Just at sunset in Meru, a herd of elephants, as if cued, passed between our eyes and the flaming western horizon, the elephants in that dense dark gray somnambulation of theirs, a sort of dream—trunks hanging, mothers gently shepherding their young, and a bull's great ears slow-motion flapping, as if he were a giant prehistoric fish finning its way through ocean depths. Then abruptly, like a theater curtain, darkness fell.

Simeon sought out the distant speck of light that he said was our campfire, and pointed the Land Cruiser toward it. Now Abyssinian nightjars discovered the magic wash of the headlight beams. They flitted in and out of the barrels of light, like dolphins frisking before a boat's prow. Then we were in full dark, except for the beacon light of camp. In 45 more minutes of bouncing across nearly open plain, we were there. Bink's crew had established a little village of tents among tamarind trees beside a narrow watercourse called the Kanjoo River.

They had pitched a kitchen tent, a dining tent, and then in a neat row like a hotel corridor between the tamarind trees, they had set up our sleeping tents with, a few feet behind each of them, a tent for latrine and shower. This was not to be—not now at least—hard living. The tented camp safari is one of the world's more civilized routines.

Binks' staff, the men brought along to set up tents, cook, and handle other logistics, numbered about half a dozen. They were mostly members of different tribes—Kikuyu, Embu, Meru, Luo, Wanderobo. They spoke to one another, and to Binks, in Swahili, the intertribal lingua franca devised by the Arab slavers in centuries past to communicate as they went in-country from the coast to do their business. It is a soft, liquid-flowing language that, when reduced to a semaphore between boss and servants, becomes a sort of pidgin that sounds musically repetitive, like bird notes.

As we pulled into camp, two members of the staff carried buckets of hot water to the shower tents. We showered, put on clean clothes, made drinks at a bar set up by the dining tent, then settled down beside the enormous campfire, which had been constructed African style—no orderly rectilinear log cabins of firewood here, but a crackling, chaotic abundance, half a tree at a time, piled on, and shooting up sparks and glowing woodflakes like a little galaxy pouring back up toward the stars.

In the morning just before dawn, there was muffled Swahili again from the camp staff—the language full of low music, its vowels and stops like a dark stream rushing over rocks.

January Wambua, a short Wakamba man, one of the cook's assistants, brought hot tea. I would hear a word of muffled Swahili outside the tent flap, and I would call, *"Karibou,"* meaning, "Come in," or "Welcome." The morning ritual was always the same.

January had nine children and enjoyed safari work, but said that he had trouble with his English. As a result, he practiced it incessantly. The first morning when he brought my tea, I thanked him, and he replied with eloquent irrelevance: "Neither a borrower nor a lender be!"

W. H. Auden, heading for Iceland years ago, wondered if a man became a different person when he went to a different place. I thought of an animal variation on that line as the African landscapes changed around us. I wondered, for example, if the elephants in the dry desert country of Samburu—a thorny expanse, land like lizard hide, like West Texas—were different somehow from those pushing through the cold, damp, dense forests thousands of feet up on the slopes of the Aberdares, in the difficult country where Mau Mau fighters hid from the British during the uprising in the 1950's. They were certainly different in my sight. The landscape frames the animals; their life is the vital flow of the scene, its movable parts.

And we had an extravagance of landscape. I sometimes wondered whether I was more attracted by the creatures or by the places where we found them—the tremendous power of the spaces, the big-boulder kopjes on volcanic moonscapes, the Rift Valley, and always bluish, promising mountains in the distance.

As we broke camp in Meru, a troop of baboons came out of the forest around us and picked through the campfire ashes, looking for food. They lurked in the trees, and then darted out on their knuckles into the clearing to search, and then dodged back furtively into the bush.

The first new landscape after Meru lay to the north, in Samburu. We set off once again for a time in the Kenya of overcrowded people and dangerous, noisy traffic.

In late morning the car broke down, and Simeon crawled underneath to find the trouble. I found a place in the shade of an olive tree and was abruptly 15 degrees cooler than I had been a moment before in the sun. Air conditioning. The Africans who passed me walking on the road—Meru and Kikuyu mostly, the men with pangas (machetes) heading for the fields of sugar cane, young goatherds with long whacking sticks to keep the animals out of traffic, a mother carrying an open umbrella to shield the baby riding on her back—watched me in roughly the way that I watched elephants. I was a curiosity.



Simeon found the trouble—dirt in the gas line, which he simply blew out—and we headed north to rendezvous with Alan Binks and Neil for lunch. We had left the farms behind and now crossed forbidding, sun-smitten, washed-out country. An apparition: in the middle of nowhere, we came upon a man riding a bicycle, pedaling laboriously through thick sandy dust, barely making headway. We left him in a cloud. We saw two jackals cross the road ahead, bounding. A goshawk was working the upper air. This seemed a more predatory country. We made a very dusty camp in a grove of whistling thorn trees (acacias)—their thorns like nails that, as Alan Binks said, could penetrate a six-ply tire.

I did not like the country much. In late afternoon, in the midst of what seemed to me remote, desolate landscape, Simeon found human tracks. But that night the sky was Edenically clear, as clear as the beginning of the world, and the new quarter-moon lay upon black velvet. The owl that had been hooting around camp earlier in the evening now was silent.

Next day we were up early to prowl. Excitement: a few yards from camp we found fresh lion tracks. They had come by during the night. In mid-morning, not far from the Ewaso Njiro River, Alan Binks discovered a leopard stalking a herd of impalas—the impalas close-grouped and anxious, the leopard nervous about our cars coming in so close upon his hunting. The impalas stood for long moments, frozen in an acacia grove, alert. But one buck seemed to be pursuing a young doe, whether to herd her out of danger or to mate I could not tell.

he landscapes have forms that are as different and fascinating as the animals. Part of the freedom one experiences there has to do with the place's huge improvisational spirit of design and possibility. Now in a day's drive we came across thorny country with dust-grayed trees beside the road, dust-grayed Turkana goatherds and gradually into greener landscape, to Timau, where we lunched on trout farmed there in the cool woods, and to Nanyuki in the shadow of Mount Kenya, then across to the Aberdares, which are, I suppose, my favorite place in Kenya, possibly not counting the Masai Mara.

The Aberdare Mountains rise from the plain and ascend through thousands of feet, beginning with shambas and small cultivations on the lower slopes, then ascending forests of olive and fig. Each new thousand feet of elevation seems a different country. The colors and vegetation in the middle elevations have a shaggy, primeval, moss-silvered secrecy about them that predates time. The bongo hides there. The bongo is an antelope that grows to the size of an eland, with reddish pelt and white stripes, so difficult to capture or even see that it has become for hunters over the years a kind of unicorn. I saw a bongo in captivity down below at the Mount Kenya Safari Club game ranch. They are said to be quite dangerous with their horns if ever cornered.

There in the middle-ranging forests of the Aberdares, one also sees trapezing colobus monkeys, flashing out of shade through sunlight into shade again, trailing their waving black-and-white long hair. Many elephants have been driven up into the Aberdares from the plains by the press of farming and sheer population. Up the winding roads one notices deep, round holes gouged out of the mountainside, beside the track. I asked Simeon what creature had made these holes. It seems that at high elevations, the elephants are unable to get the minerals in their diet that they need, so they have to dig in the dirt with their tusks for minerals to eat. The holes make the road look as if it had been a scene of battle, with cannonballs pounding into the hillsides: an almost comic effect, for elephant dung looks like cannonballs. And so a little part of the landscape resembles some strange 18th-century battlefield where behemoths fought.

We broke out of the forest at last into upland meadows at an elevation of 11,000 or 12,000 feet. The air was chilly and clean in late afternoon. At one turning of the road, we came upon an immense herd of Cape buffalo, it seemed 30 or 40 of them, their great dark bodies wallowing in a sea of yellow flowers and green grasses.

The Aberdares keep changing. Now they looked like Vermont. We crawled up the rough road in four-wheel drive. And then abruptly, in the middle of Vermont, found waterbucks and more Cape buffalo, and once or twice a leopard. Around a bend an immense elephant, walking alone, with a completely stiff right foreleg. Simeon thought he might have been shot by poachers down below.

And here are white hyena droppings deposited on dark, wet rock: the droppings white because the hyena eat so many bones.

We became fascinated by the strides of animals, by their gaits and body language. One of the creatures' charms is that each is unmistakably itself: the elephant is primal elephant and nothing else, the lion is utterly lion, and so on. The creature's stride declares a personality, as vivid and distinctive as its horns and striping, or its style of hunting and being hunted.

In late morning in Meru, for example: the Nyambeni Hills rose blue-purple in the distance to the west above a vast flat of dun-colored grasses. In the middle distance, smoke from honey-hunters' tree-fires rose and plumed slowly in the emptiness.

Just inside the park we found Thommies—Thomson's gazelles. Five of them lifted their heads with that electric alertness they have, their tails switching back and forth like windshield wipers at the fastest setting, the one for rainstorms. Beyond the Thommies, three giraffes (mother, child, adolescent) were feeding upon acacia buds. They froze at our approach—impassive statuary in profile, not deigning to look at us—then in a dream-like slow-motion turned, as if rotating slowly upon their common pedestal, and galloped away. Or rather, they undulated away, their gait a sort of liquid wave moving continuously—sinuously—from head to hindquarters. The giraffe is delicate, intelligent, and eccentric, and as Karen Blixen said, "such a lady."

Minutes later we came upon six waterbucks, much larger than Thommies. When they ran, they sprang like bouncy old buggies, receding with a graceful boing-boing-boing. Then we saw zebras, with their short, round haunches, their air of amiable, extroverted power—healthy, obscurely erotic critters with a quick and thundering run.

I became a connoisseur of animal runs and walks and stillnesses. The landscape stands in motionless tableau at midday. Abruptly, danger fires through a herd like an electron, and the still creatures jolt to a quivering alertness. If scent says the danger is close enough, then all explode away for a moment or two, then stop, as if they had lost the thought somehow. The fleeing impulse dies away, and the animals return to grazing as if the instant before had been five centuries before, or had never happened. It is this dreaminess of time that I love so much among the animals.

They often move in a deep slow motion, as if traversing another medium, previous to air, and thicker—an Atlantis of time. The elephant goes sleeping that way across the spaces. The medium through which it moves might be time itself, a thicker, slower time than humans inhabit, a prehistoric metabolism.

For days in Masai Mara, we watched the wildebeests. Ungainly and pewter-colored, they are subject to sudden electric jolts of panic, to adrenal bursts of motion that can make them seem half crazed as a tribe. Now they were engaged not so much in migration as in vagrancy, wandering across the plain on strange but idiotically determined vectors. Wildebeests smell monsters on the afternoon breeze, take sudden fear and bolt for Tanzania or Uganda or the Indian Ocean—anywhere to get away.

Sometimes, of course, the monsters are there. The veldt is littered with the corpses that the lion or cheetah has killed and dined on. But sometimes the herding wildebeests seem to be caught in a collective shallow madness. A fantasy of terror shoots through a herd, and they are all gone: hysteria of hooves. The wildebeests thunder by the thousands across rivers and plains, moving like a barbarian invasion. They follow their instinct for the rains, for better grass. And they mow the grass before them. If they know where rain is, the wildebeests are relentless. Otherwise they march with an undirected rigor, without destination, like cadets on punishment, beating a trail in the parade ground. The wildebeest's bisonlike head is too large for its body, its legs too thin and ungainly. It looks like a middle-aged hypochondriac, paltry in the loins and given to terrible anxiety attacks, the sort of creature whose hands (if it had hands) would be clammy. God's genius for design may have faltered with the wildebeest.

In Masai Mara, vultures wheel dreamily in the air, like a slow-motion tornado of birds. Below the swirling tunnel a cheetah has brought down a baby wildebeest. The cheetah, loner and fleet aristocrat, the upper-class version of the hyena, has opened up the wildebeest and devoured the internal organs. The cheetah's belly is swollen and its mouth is ringed with blood as it breathes heavily with the exertion of gorging. A dozen vultures flap down to take their turn. They wait 20 yards away, then waddle in a little toward the kill to test the cheetah. The cheetah, in a burst, rushes the vultures to drive them off, and then returns to the baby wildebeest. The vultures grump and readjust their feathers and wait their turn, the surly lumpen-carrion class.

The skeleton of an elephant lies out in the grasses near a baobab tree and a scattering of black volcanic stones. The thick-trunked gnarled baobab gesticulates with its branches, as if trying to summon help. There are no tusks among the bones, of course; ivory vanishes quickly in East Africa. The elephant is three weeks dead. Poachers. Not far away, a baby elephant walks alone. That is unusual. Elephants are careful mothers and do not leave their young unattended. The skeleton is the mother, and the baby is the orphan.

One day in Meru our Land Cruiser glides through the lion-colored grasses. It is late afternoon, and lions everywhere are rising from their long day's slumber to think about hunting. Simeon sees the lion and stops and points. Poking my head like a periscope through the roof of the cruiser, I squint, trying to build the platonic lion out of grass. Still the lion will not come. The beast is hidden in the grass like the number in the dot test for color blindness. Rake your gaze into the grass, staring deeply into it, and slowly the scene develops like a Polaroid picture, taking color and form. Your eyes discover that they are staring straight, deeply, into the eyes of a lion—only the eyes. And the lion is staring straight and deeply back. The eyes in the grass are yellow-black eyes, cat's eyes, emitting rays of measurement and judgment and hunger. I feel the chill of a savage attention. At last the Polaroid develops itself fully. The lion turns and lies in full view, spreading the beige grass and lying precisely in the posture of the woman in the grass in Andrew Wyeth's painting "Christina's World." The grasses in Wyeth's dream and the grasses garnishing the lion have the same color and texture. But whereas Wyeth's Christina was crippled and lies in an unforgettable posture of longing, of groping, the lion, his hindquarters lazing off to one side, is a masterwork of indolent power.

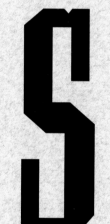

ome friends arranged for me to have lunch with a Masai elder in the Lord Delamere Dining Room of the Norfolk. The elder, Moses, lived a six-hour drive—or a four-day walk for a Masai—from Nairobi. But he had done occasional fieldwork with American ornithologists and animal behaviorists. He spoke English. And when he came to Nairobi, he wore sneakers and a couple of sweatshirts and dark trousers, and more or less fit in for a day or two before he returned to the Loita Hills.

The Masai consider themselves to be superior to other creatures on earth. They tolerate Americans and Europeans as amusing characters with interesting toys—digital watches, Polaroids, automobiles, and so on.

I asked Moses what he dreamed about. My friend hosting the lunch thought this an odd question. Moses seemed to find it perfectly normal. I asked him if he had nightmares about the animals. He said: "Oh, no, I have nightmares about Nairobi—nightmares about speeding cars and bright lights and lorries crashing. And all the noise of a thousand radios playing!" He made a face and clutched his head: "All of that noise crashing out of the air!" In the Loita Hills, said Moses, "we sing, but we sing without instruments. It makes some sense."

So everyone has a different idea of dangerous wildlife. As the conservationist David Western said, "For Kenyans, the frontier is the city."

Moses laughed at the folly of Nairobi. He picked at the plate of fruit that he had taken from the buffet. He said that he was eager to get out of the city, away from cars and paved roads. Most of all, back to his cattle. The Masai's cattle are everything to him—wealth, sustenance, home itself, a kind of sweet, slow-moving animate raison d'être that he tends and cherishes, whose daily grazing and watering and wandering become the organizing principles of Masai life.

Once, much later, I asked Moses how many cows he owns. I did not realize the question was impolite. I discovered that the Masai do not like to enumerate. On seeing the herd, I guessed that Moses owned about 100 cows. I learned that he knew each cow individually, its markings, its idiosyncrasies, its personality, knew which cow would lead the herd on the day's march to grazing, and which cow would bring up the rear.

The Masai live and work and graze their cows among the wild animals—at least those Masai still fortunate enough to live out in the bush, self-sustaining, practicing their traditions. Many of them have been forced into jobs, into towns, into Nairobi. The government has tried to make them settle down. It has forbidden many of the warrior practices, such as cattle raiding. But the lucky Masai still live remote from authority, wearing only the chuka, a kind of bright toga draped over one shoulder (the Masai refer to anyone who wears trousers as "he who would imprison his farts"), and they herd their cows every day over the same rough territory they share with lions, hyenas, zebras, warthogs, jackals, gerenuks, Thomson's gazelles, elands, and the rest.

The Masai attitude toward the animals is friendly and pragmatic. The Masai take a sort of detached, aesthetic view of any creature that is no threat. Children are taught an appropriate fear of lions and leopards and buffalo and rhinos—although the rhinos have now been poached to the vanishing point. Each Masai male old enough to herd goats carries a spear, *rungu* (a short club about the length of a man's forearm, which may also be thrown as a weapon, end-over-end) and a walking stick, or rather, a goat-rump-swatting stick. Rungu and walking stick are often carved of olive wood, which has a sweet heavy density and ages to the smoothness of yellowed ivory. Before a boy is circumcised and becomes a warrior, he is taught not to fight the lion, but to yell and make noise to try to scare the predator off from the cattle, and after that to run and get help. Some lions have a pronounced taste for beef, and so the danger of lions to Masai herds is roughly like the threat of predators to expensive cars parked on the streets of New York City with radio and tape player inside: a temptation.

To Masai warriors, of course the lion is a measure of manhood. In the preliminaries to becoming a warrior at age 15 or so, the young man is supposed to spend the night in the bush, alone and unarmed. The night in the bush of Africa has metaphysical implications of darkness, terror, and the unknown. Practically speaking, it is the time when the predators go out to hunt, especially when the moon is full and the prey are naked in the pale light of the plain. The boy's greatest danger on that initiation night is the lion.

Moses introduced me to Taiko Turia, a gangling, somewhat sullen boy who was about to become a warrior. Did the boy look forward to it? He spoke only Masai, but Moses translated his reply. I thought Moses colored the answer a little, making it more heroic: "I will be a warrior and have beautiful hair and live in the forest with the lions, and sometimes fight with them. I will get more cows. I will not be a baby anymore. I will go on cattle raids. And fight!" In answer to my question, he said: "No, I have not killed a lion—yet!" Moses beamed at that *yet!* The answering boy still looked doubtful. I asked the boy, about to be circumcised, to draw a picture of a lion for me, and he took my ballpoint pen and in my notebook drew me a savage Leo *dentato,* a beast with mouth open and horrible sharp teeth. Back in Nairobi weeks later, I ran into a psychologist and showed it to him. He laughed and said: "Obvious, isn't it?"

It is against the law in Kenya now to hunt lions. The Masai still do so, but they don't talk about it, and if confronted with the evidence, they plead self-defense—the lion was attacking them or the herd.

All the animals seem to be afraid of Masai, including lions. The knowledge that they inspire awe as they lope splendidly across the countryside in their beadwork, and the dreamy arrogance that is a trait of the tribe, endow the Masai with a lord-of-creation detachment.

The warrior bravado may become hilarious or sad when infected by externals. An English-born Kenyan told me the story of Masai men who sold their spears to insistent tourists, then used the windfall money to buy beer. They got drunk and decided to go on a lion hunt, but now had only one child's spear. Several of the men were badly mauled by a lion in the drunken moonlight, but they survived: an African O. Henry story.

When we had lunch at the Norfolk, Moses told me that he had killed seven lions. Moses speaks with a kind of commanding modesty and matter-of-factness. I was never sure what to make of the claim of seven lions. I was inclined to believe it, but it occurred to me that Moses meant to entertain me. He also told me later, as we herded cattle in the Loita Hills, that he had killed a dozen or two Cape buffalo. He may have seen it as his duty as a host to humor my fantasies of adventure and danger there in the hills.

Now, sitting in the Lord Delamere Dining Room of the Norfolk Hotel, Moses solemnly explained to me that all animals are left-handed. It is true, said Moses. Never get onto a lion's left side. A lion attacks from his left. All animals instinctively lead with the left paw, the left hoof, the left horn. Even cows are left-handed.

There were holes in Moses' earlobes where ornaments might fit, but they were austerely empty. Handsome, thoughtful, impassive, Moses conjured up wild animals. His gaze was sleepy and distant.

n the table, Moses demonstrated how the rhinoceros thinks. He used the salt shaker to represent me. The pepper shaker would be the rhino. The sugar bowl would be the boulder that stood between me and the rhino. "Be careful," Moses warned. He moved the rhino in an ominous drift to its left. The rhino began to circle the sugar bowl, using the bowl as cover to ambush the salt shaker, me, from behind. I became a naked and oblivious wanderer on the white linen plain. I stood frozen and defenseless as the rhino came on.

"Rhinos will always go to the left, like this," said Moses softly. He knocked down the salt shaker with a sharp crack of the pepper shaker, like a chess master toppling the king. I went down. White grains of salt spilled out of the holes at the top of my head, and I expired on the flat white linen.

To get to Moses' *enk'ang* (small village) in the Loita Hills, the Land Cruiser travels for three hours over paved road to the dusty frontier town of Narok, then follows a rutted washboard road across an empty and chokingly dusty plain until it shifts into four-wheel drive and begins the slow climb into the hills. It is lovely in the hills. They look somewhat like the Sangre de Cristo Mountains of New Mexico. Part of their beauty is their pristine remoteness. One rarely encounters a white man there. (That is an interesting phenomenon, the European or American visitor's aversion to seeing others like himself: encountering someone like oneself damages the illusion that one has escaped and gone into the wild.)

I came first to the enk'ang of Moses' older brother, Joseph, who, surrounded by children and dogs and friends, strode out from the *boma,* a tall thorn-and-cedar enclosure, the feudal African fortress against lions and leopards. Joseph was smaller and more delicately boned than Moses. He had the fine, intelligent head of a Talmudic scholar, I decided, an Ethiopian head, a fastidious head, given to complex distinctions. Joseph and I set out in the evening light to walk across the hills to Moses' boma. Joseph wore a handsome red blanket over his shoulder and, oddly, a suede golf cap that suited him well. He was barefoot, his feet tough and thick as they trod upon rocks and twigs and thorns and dung indifferently.

I asked Joseph if there were many wild animals close by. He was not carrying a spear just now, only a thin wand of olive wood. The spear was not necessary at this time of day between bomas, Joseph explained. People passed back and forth; the lions would stay away.

Joseph talked, when asked, about the Masai diet. Milk; tea; some maize; goat or beef on special occasions. Do Masai ever eat the wild animals? Joseph answered: "Sometimes we eat the gazelle, because the gazelle is close to God."

Joseph's accent had a strange geographical range, with pronunciations in English that sounded as if they had come from either India or Germany. God came out sounding like the German *Gott.*

I gave a sigh of discovery. "Ah." Long pause.

"Are there other animals that the Masai consider to be close to God?" I had decided, in vague tracery, that the gazelle's grace was associated in the Masai mind with God's grace, a profound though punning link, and that by eating the flesh of the gazelle, the Masai thought to partake of the grace of God. A pagan chinging of the altar bells: a transubstantiation.

I walked on through the hills, my hands behind me like an abbot. Then I glanced up at Joseph and saw that the elder was looking at me in consternation.

"Close to God?" asked Joseph.

"You said the gazelle is close to God," I prompted. Something in Joseph detonated minutely, and then he waved it off with a snort.

"Oh, no! I said that we eat gazelle because it is close to *goat!* The gazelle tastes like goat! We like goat!"

Gott and goat. It was a lesson learned. East Africans see no spiritual significance in the animals, even though each of the Masai clans claims an unsentimental relationship with one animal or another.

One night around a fire inside the boma, Moses recounted some of his dreams. In one of them, he runs up a ravine with steep rock walls on three sides, pursued by a rhino. He claws at the rock walls, trying to escape, hanging by his fingertips. He wakes up screaming. In another dream, a lion is dragging Moses through deep grass. Moses desperately clutches at the grass with his fingers, but the grass comes up in clumps, and Moses is dragged on.

The pen where Moses and his family kept their goats at night was covered with a grid of heavy wire. When I wondered about it, Moses explained, "Leopard comes at night to take the goats." Around every Masai enk'ang is built a sturdy fence of thorn and cedar to keep the lions out. One day, walking in the forest, Moses shouldered an enormous slab of cedar to add to his boma. "The lion makes me do a lot of work," he remarked. Sometimes the barricades do not hold, and the Masai wake to the bawl and crashing of cattle as the lion struggles to carry off his beef.

Reality and dreams dance around to bite each other. One night, when Joseph was still a boy, he and his friend dreamed the same dream, about a leopard attacking the calves. "We both woke up at the same time, screaming and fighting the leopard," Joseph said. "We both roared like the leopard, and then the whole boma woke up screaming"—shouting about the leopard the boys had seen—but had seen only in their dreams. And in the morning, by the goats' pen, the people found leopard tracks. "You know," Joseph said thoughtfully, "there are scary animals. And they eat people. Sometimes people never learn to be brave, and even as old men, they are still afraid."

Moses arranged for me to meet the witch doctor, a *laibon*, or medicine man, named Ole Loompirai. He came at dusk and sat talking to me in a dark, dung-walled hut. I offered him Tusker beer that I had brought up in the Land Cruiser from Narok, and he drank it by the bottle, quickly, as he told me about his work. As he spoke about charms and animal sacrifices, we could hear through the tiny window of the hut the voice of my driver, Davis, a middle-aged Luo from Lake Victoria who considered himself a Roman Catholic priest. Davis carried a notebook inscribed with the text of the Latin mass, copied from a missal he had borrowed somewhere in his travels. Davis sometimes donned a long white alb and, all by himself outside the boma, performed services beside his Land Rover, chanting the Latin in a rich bass.

Davis was at his evening prayers as I talked to the witch doctor, and Latin poured through the window: *"Pater noster qui es in coelis, sanctificetur nomen tuum...."* The laibon explained the uses of animals in his work. He employed the warthog, for example, to cast a spell to keep the government out of Masai business. The laibon used a dik-dik, that small, lovely antelope, to thwart someone's plans. It works thus: he places charms upon the animal and then releases it in the direction of the person who is the target of the spell. For help with childbirth, he drapes the skin of an eland on the woman, the eland being much like the cow, which possesses magic powers. In order to bring rain, the laibon places a dead frog on the ground, belly up, with a charm upon it. Within twenty-four hours, before the frog decays, the rain will fall.

The laibon drained his Tusker and asked for another. From outside, in the failing light: *"Ecce agnus Dei. Ecce qui tollis peccata mundi."* Of course it all works, said the laibon, irritated that the doubting question was asked. If there are sick cattle, sacrifice a sheep, and take the undigested grass out of its stomach, stretch the skin over the entrance to the boma. The cattle will pass beneath the skin and grass, which will draw the illness out of the cows.

Asked if he liked the wild animals, the laibon answered: "I like the animals but they do not like human beings. That is the problem. But the eland is a friend. You can eat an eland, and use his skin for many things. Not long ago the laibon dreamed that a spitting cobra bit him. He cried in his sleep and leaped out of bed shaking, and awoke.

The laibon has been chased by lions many times. The worst attack came one evening when he was walking to another enk'ang to see his girlfriend. (I savored the idea of a witch doctor going to pick up his girlfriend for a date.) The lion stalked and menaced him for a long distance, the laibon jabbing with his spear, the lion never quite attacking. Odd.

**D**reaming: Shirley Strum says that there came a time when the baboons spoke to her in English. They came to her in her dreams and asked for her help. For 12 years Strum, an anthropologist from California, had been studying a baboon troop at a ranch called Kekopey, near Gilgil. Then the ranch was turned into an agricultural collective, and the new farmers menaced the baboons and tried to kill them off.

The baboons were Strum's friends. She had given all of them names, and she sat among them every day. They were accustomed to her and accepted her. She came among them like a ghostly premonition of their evolutionary future, a benevolent spirit out of the time warp, another civilization. She came from space. She sat among them, holding her clipboard, and made silent notes.

Strum understood the dangers of anthropomorphism, of coming to love the animals too much and to hate the people endangering them. Strum, the least violent of creatures, said that if she had had a gun, she might have shot the farmers threatening the baboons. Now, in Shirley Strum's dreams, the baboons asked her for help, and she searched for a ranch that would accept them. The ranchers mostly thought she was insane. Baboons raid crops. Importing baboons to a ranch made as much sense as transplanting cockroaches to a New York City apartment. But at last Strum made an arrangement with the Chololo Ranch on the Laikipia Plateau north of Nairobi. She had the baboons trapped and sedated and brought to a new home where they would be safe, and she went on silently studying them.

"Watching the baboons is like watching a soap opera," Strum said, "except that the baboons are much nicer people than you see on *Dallas* or *Dynasty*." I walked out with Strum among the baboons at 8:00 A.M. in

Laikipia. They were feeding on the buds of an acacia tree not far from the granite kopje where they slept. Strum knew all the baboons. "That is C.J. and Ron," she began. "The female is Zilla. C.J. and Ron have a conflict of emotions." Ron was new to the troop, and so was Ndofu.

Baboon life, Strum said, is an endless series of negotiations. The drama of their lives revolved not around sex or male intimidation but around alliances, around friendships. Baboons have a Japanese complexity of deferences and dominances. They live, it seemed to a newcomer, in a constant state of distracted tension, as if caught in an elastic web of attractions and repulsions, a web constantly in motion, in adjustment of distances. I studied their hands, which were so human, so adept and articulate, that they could be trained for neurosurgery, if good hands were all a neurosurgeon needed.

Now a magic evening light came cross the Laikipia Plateau, and the baboons straggled in from their day's browsings among the acacia flowers. They sat and socialized on the lower rocks of their high kopje, grooming one another with a sweet absorption, playing with their babies. Like almost everyone and everything in Africa, they seemed profoundly tribal. Another troop of baboons arrived, a hundred yards away, and each tribe stared at the other with a nervous intensity across the evening light.

The East Africa of the animals is a paradise, but one capable of ominous effects: nature's sweet morning, but also an awful mess, a killing field. The peaceable kingdom is dung-covered and bone-littered, its graceful life subject to sudden violent extinctions. A high turnover. Life is to be stalked and slain, almost abstractly, and ingested. These days the death is also to be photographed. The tourist minibuses cluster around a cheetah kill. The late 20th century suckles forlornly on the Pleistocene. Visitors, popping through the roofs of the vehicles like blossoms from a vase, will glare at one another with the hatred of one whose dream has been interrupted.

Among the wild animals, individual life has no claims. What matters is something collective, the species, the tribe, the march of genes, the drive of life, and its dreamlike indifference to the details of individual death. The Great Chain of Eating. Nature at this level is bloody and sloppy, faintly horrifying and very beautiful.

Life and death coexist with a unique ecological compactness. Nothing is wasted. First the lion dines, and then the hyena, and then the vulture, and then the lesser specialists, insects and the like, until the carcass is picked utterly clean, and what is left, bones and horns, subsides into the grass. It has been an African custom to take the dead out into the open and leave them unceremoniously for the hyenas.

The conservationist David Western, whom his friends call Jonah, flies his Cessna south over Amboseli, toward the snow-covered dome of Mount Kilimanjaro. He flies low toward a dry, alkaline lake bottom. Jonah Western, a distinguished practical joker, has been known to load his plane with cannonballs of elephant dung (fairly newly dropped, he says, well crusted on the outside but still mushy inside) and make low-flying bombing runs over the camps of other naturalists.

At the edge of the lake, a herd of elephants moves like a dense gray cloud, slow-motion, in lumbering solidity: a mirage of floating boulders. Around them dust devils rise spontaneously out of the desert, little tornadoes that swirl up on the thermals and go jittering and rushing among the animals busy in the primal garden.

Jonah Western's father was killed by a rogue elephant years ago in Tanzania. Western has devoted his career to understanding and trying to save the wildlife. He is not necessarily elegiac about the prospects, does not entirely believe some African version of the Turner thesis—the end of frontier. Western and his wife, Shirley Strum, place their hopes in the economic argument for preserving the animals. They believe that an emergent African middle class will take the lead in protecting the wild animals because they are an economic resource, the indispensable magnet for tourism. The animals, in other words, may earn their own keep—may be spared because enlightened governments realize that the creatures are profitably picturesque. Whatever works.

The wild animals date back at least 2 million years. They represent, we imagine, the first order of creation, and they are vividly marked with God's eccentric genius of design: life poured into pure forms, life unmitigated by complexities of consciousness, language, ethics, premeditation, free will. A wild animal does not contradict its own nature, does not thwart itself, as man endlessly does. A wild animal never plays for the other side. The wild animals are a holiday from deliberation. They are sheer life. To see a bright being that lives without thought is, to the complex, cross-grained human mind, profoundly liberating.

# ELEPHANTS

The elephant has an aura of dreamlike intelligence that belongs almost to a different order of creation. The great gray wrinkled mass, we think, conceals some knowledge. Elephants are lumbering paradoxes: funny, messy as they knock down trees, swayingly graceful, terrifying when angry. And somehow more kingly than the lion. The poachers who kill them for the ivory are committing regicide, as if Babar were the last of the Romanovs.

These elephants were among the acacia and olive trees just below Mount Kilimanjaro in Amboseli. It was late morning, and the equatorial sun was still climbing. In that strong, harsh light I used a polarizing filter to separate out the highlights of the sky, the mountain, and the sun gleaming off the tusks.

85mm lens
with polarizing filter

I like to use foregrounds when I can, sometimes to frame the animal in its natural camouflage. In this picture, shot in Samburu, I simply framed the elephant in the setting of its lunch. Keeping a safe distance of about 100 feet, I used a relatively short telephoto lens and played peekaboo with the elephant as it enjoyed an unhurried meal of doum palm leaves. I shot away, and every so often would see an eye, an ear, sometimes the whole head of the animal popping through the fronds.

180mm lens

When we left camp before dawn, the air still sharp and cold, the grasses wet enough with dew to soak our pant legs, the animals would already be awake and stirring.

They would start their grazing as the sun began to warm the plain.

Fujica 617

300mm lens

300mm lens

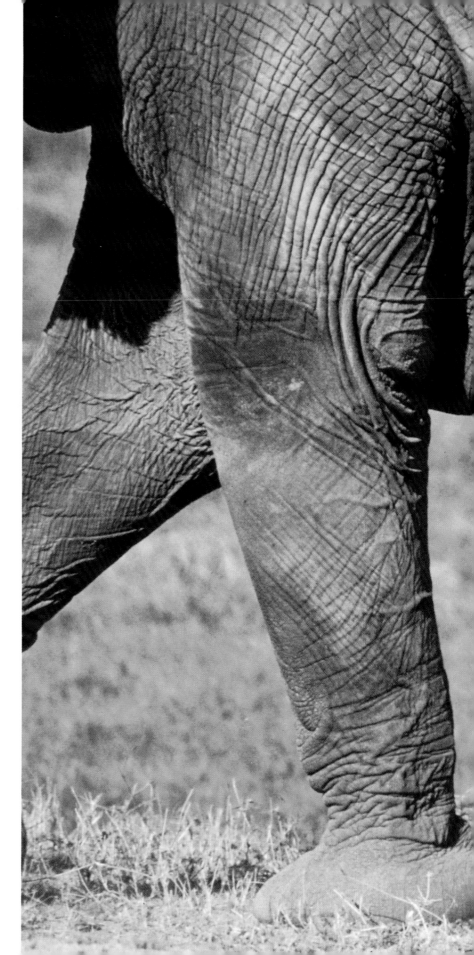

Part of the pleasure of a photo safari is the sheer unpredictability of the hunt, of sliding through the wild countryside—through tall grasses, past acacias and baobab trees and doum palms, or across black-bouldered, almost lunar landscapes—and waiting for the animals to disclose themselves. Ninety percent of the photographs in this book presented themselves in that spontaneous way. This picture, however, which is one of my favorites, was one that I carried with me mentally from New York. I knew that, with luck, I would get it. I spotted these elephants heading for a crossing of the Mara River. I asked my guide to drive the Land Cruiser parallel at the same speed they were walking, staying about 100 feet away so as not to alarm them. Then the mother elephant and her baby reproduced the image I had pictured before the safari began.

300mm lens

Elephants are among the planet's best mothers, and so it is relatively rare to see a baby walking by itself, outside its mother's immediate orbit. In this case, however, as we drove along a ridgeline in the Aberdares, I looked down into a flowered meadow and saw this baby wandering a bit. Perhaps the elephants feel more secure within the protection of the mountain forests than they do below, on the comparatively bare plains, and therefore have a more relaxed attitude toward child care. They are certainly less susceptible to poachers. In fact, many of the Aberdare elephants were driven up there by the press of human beings below. Their sense of security on this high ground gave me a chance to take this unusual picture of a baby by itself.

400mm lens

300mm lens (both)

The last pictures of the day are sometimes the most wonderful and, oddly enough, the easiest to take. You simply find the most handsome setting in which to watch the animals as they march across the African sunset, which is almost always stunning. In this case, about half an hour before sundown as we headed back toward camp, I noticed a large group of elephants in the far distance, moving across the plain on a vector that I saw would draw them across the sun just as it was sliding into the horizon. I waited, and the elephants came on. As with all sunset pictures, I bracketed the exposures so as to get a range from dark to light. This allows me to select the best image later—in the process of editing rather than in the act of shooting.

180mm lens

The giraffe would be merely bizarre and ungainly if it were not so undulatingly graceful in motion. The strange, towering design gives the giraffe a sort of abstracted serenity, the animal's small head waving on its long, lithe stem like a heliotrope. The giraffe's vision, keen for miles across the plain, endows it with an air of peaceful detachment.

# GIRAFFES

G iraffes keep track of one another for miles across the open plain, and as a result, they don't often look gregarious. Their idea of being close may be half a mile or more. You don't see large groups of them together very often. I was delighted early one morning in Meru, just after sunrise, when I came upon this spectacular assembly arrayed in the glow of the first light.

600mm lens

**I** looked down from a ridge to see this giraffe drinking from the Mara River. Then I noticed the zebra above him on the bank, the two animals seeming to follow the graceful lead of the same conductor. I sometimes use a shorter lens to try to capture the surrounding landscape. After I shot the picture, I wondered about the sheer physics of being a giraffe. How does the drinking animal get the water up that long slope of neck into its stomach?

180mm lens

300mm lens

**S**ometimes Amboseli looks like a ruined garden. The trees in the foreground were knocked down by elephants, notoriously messy eaters that devastate sections of forest when they do not have enough territory over which to range. On this late morning I used a polarizing filter for this picture of giraffes crossing the plains. A cloud-filled sky may make a late-morning picture in the way that the sun makes superb sunrise and sunset photos. One trick when using a polarizing filter is to test the scene with your sunglasses to decide whether or not to use the polarizer. If the clouds really pop out and the scene looks more dramatic, then it will look that way with the filter on the lens. If the scene looks better without sunglasses, then shoot it without the polarizing filter. I always try to shoot it both ways.

135mm lens

I suppose that if a giraffe were watching a man eating with a knife and fork, the giraffe might wonder how that feat could be accomplished without all kinds of puncture wounds and bloodshed. A natural question. The giraffe displays an equally baffling talent for casually eating the buds from an acacia tree without injuring tongue and lips on lethal thorns that can puncture a six-ply tire.

800mm lens

# BEASTS

The animals seem to organize themselves into categories of lightness and heaviness. Some are quick and frisky. Others move with a thick, glowering solidity, like storm clouds. It is a mistake, however, to assume the cloud will not move quickly. The cape buffalo, the rhino, even the hippo can erupt in amazing bursts of speed, their sullenness suddenly gone all electric.

OnE morning as
we followed the bank at
a bend of the Mara
River, we came upon
this companionable
pileup: nearly 100
hippos nuzzling
together like puppies.
The river teems with an
amazing variety of life,
including crocodiles the
size (it seems) of ocean-
going yachts.

300mm lens

**B**ig edition and small edition: Later I found this mother and child on the banks of the Mara River, on their way to join the main herd cooling itself in midstream.

400mm lens

600mm lens

400mm lens

300mm lens

600mm lens (both)

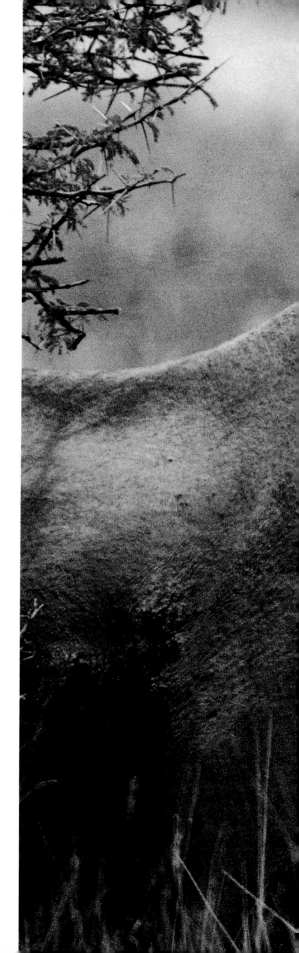

The rhino has no natural enemies. Its only predator is man—who is predator enough. The black rhino has been poached to the brink of extinction. The disgusting part is that the beast, a remnant of the Pleistocene epoch, is being hunted off the face of the earth for the sake of its horn (actually made of densely compacted hair), which is ground up and sold in the Orient as a tonic that is supposed to cure various aches and ailments.

I spotted this massive Cape buffalo standing in a meadow in the Aberdares in late morning, and as I watched through an 800mm lens, a bright little oxpecker landed on his head and began policing the insect life there. The buffalo and the oxpecker have a good relationship, mutually beneficial.

800mm lens

**T**he wildebeest migration is one of the most spectacular events on earth. Tens of thousands of wildebeests (otherwise known as gnus) make a dramatic forced march across vast expanses of East Africa in search of water and grasses.

Fujica 617

**Y**ou begin to notice social patterns among the animals. Zebras and wildebeests, for example, enjoy one another's company. They intermingle while grazing out on the plain, then wander together to the water for their evening drink. I saw these wildebeests and zebras lined up at the Mara River. A watering place, of course, is one of the surest locations to find a variety of game. The lion knows this as well, which may explain the tight arrangement of the animals here.

300mm lens

I caught up with the migration one day at the Mara River. The animals spent hours nerving themselves to plunge in and struggle across. Wildebeests trying to make up their minds look like an enormous experiment in mob psychology. This is probably more trying for the photographer waiting for the shot than for the animals themselves. For a long time they simply milled around, undecided.

180mm lens

T hen one of the wildebeests, a leader, at last launched himself into the swift-flowing brown-green water. After him, more and more took courage and in a headlong tumble plunged in and humped and clawed their way across.

89

300mm lens

**S**ometimes the migration resembles a Texas cattle drive. The wildebeests are skittish and given to stampeding at the slightest scent of lion on the wind. In this case, the herd had approached the Mara River, then got spooked by Masai cattle in the distance being driven to water by their herdboys.

The wildebeests had been about to plunge, but now wheeled around and thundered back up the bank. With many animal pictures you get only one chance. But the wildebeests have a habit of mindless repetition, so if you miss the first time, wait around.

180mm lens

They have all kinds of qualities, good and bad, that are cousin to the human—by turns quizzical, endearing, disgusting, larcenous. Baboons have the social life of a slightly messy soap opera. With baboons and monkeys we think: here is wildlife with fingers and thumbs—manipulators in several of the human meanings of the word, with wits and a consciousness that intermingles with basic instincts.

# MONKEYS

The monkey presents a technical problem for the photographer. Characteristically, a monkey is either in midair when you first see him—swinging from tree to tree like Tarzan, hard to shoot unless your reflexes are instantaneous—or else is sitting high on a limb in relative darkness, shaded by the tree, while the background sky above him is bright. But this black-faced vervet at Lake Nakuru was as well lighted as the background.

600mm lens

**W**e went to Lake Nakuru to photograph the famous flamingos there. One morning I came upon another black-faced vervet and her baby. I took care to stay far enough away so as not to spook her and used a long lens. These monkeys are so dark, you must be careful not to underexpose the photograph.

600mm lens

**A**frican farmers view baboons as crop-raiding pests with no redeeming value whatsoever. And baboons, darting and furtive, do sometimes seem like thieving parodies of human beings. But they have other almost-human qualities that are more attractive and sometimes, like this mother and baby, irresistible.

600mm lens

U p in the Aberdares, landscape and foliage and animal life seem to change radically with every thousand feet of elevation, rising out of dusty plain through thick forests of olive, bamboo, and fig until they reach 12,000 feet or so and look like windswept Scottish moorlands. Halfway up the Aberdares, in the sort of forest where Mau Mau guerrillas once hid out during their uprising in the 1950's, I spotted this regal colobus monkey.

800mm lens

# GRACE

Does beauty perform a Darwinian function in promoting the interests of some animals? Or is it just a matter of lucky accident? In any case, many of the beautiful animals still flourish—the various antelopes, for example, that are masterpieces of curve and proportion. Nature is not always an aesthetic idealist, of course. Consider the slouching, disreputable hyena or the strutty warthog, both of which are prospering as well.

The gerenuk, a small, delicate antelope about the size of a young deer, has unusual eating habits—it browses as well as grazes. On a hot plain in Samburu, I saw this improbable spectacle: the animal on its hind legs, nipping at acacia buds. The gerenuk's posture is always surprising, no matter how often you see it, and looks to be an unnatural learned trick, like a dog dancing.

300mm lens

104

Two male Thomson's gazelles, grazing impassively on Masai Mara, jolted upright when my vehicle approached. We watched each other for a moment. Then they lost interest in me, or else they were seized by an impulse to perform. So they locked horns and sparred—whether playfully or in earnest, I could not tell. They went on for five minutes. I went on for two rolls.

400mm lens

Dik-dik are tiny antelopes that look like oversized field mice. For the photographer's purposes they belong to the category of animals that demand, shoot first, think later. Remember that the original meaning of "snapshot" was a bullet fired off by reflex, without aim or premeditation. We were crawling slowly down a track in the Mara, just before an afternoon rain closed in, when I spotted this pair among the weeds. I didn't think, but twisted the lens to a rapid focus and fired.

600mm lens

The light was
perfect—the very first
light pouring out of the
crack of dawn, flowing
across the Masai Mara,
backlighting every
detail. Those first 15 or
20 minutes after the
sun comes up usually
produce the best
pictures of the day. I
got this impala picture
in that magic interval.
Taken an hour later,
the same photograph
would have looked flat
and ordinary.

300mm lens

Occasionally an animal will submit to having a formal portrait made. This impala at Meru stared straight back at my lens with a kind of frank, aristocratic curiosity. Then he even struck some poses, turning his head this way and that, before returning to full face.

600mm lens

S ilver-backed jackals are more attractive than hyenas, but they are in the same line of work—hunting in packs, running down the weaker prey (injured Thommies or baby zebras or such), or else taking leftovers after the lion or cheetah has dined. When jackals and hyenas have had their meal, the vultures follow up. I found these jackals taking their ease on a termite mound in Samburu. When they saw me, they came alert with the predator's natural riveted attention. They decided I was not their meat, and in another instant, they were gone.

600mm lens

L ike the wildebeest, the zebra is a great deliberator when it comes to a decision about river crossings. Here on the Mara River, I waited for an hour while a herd considered. The zebra is lion's prey, of course, but is a fast animal with lethal hooves and powerful hindquarters. When fighting, the zebra bites or else uses a fierce swiveling lateral hind-kick that is murder to its enemies. But the swift river is an alien element for zebras. It took this herd a while to talk themselves into crossing. Sometimes it pays the photographer to be patient and wait out the animals' hesitations.

180mm lens

**H**uman Kenyans ride in a taxi called a *matatu*, which screams along the crumbling asphalt roads at breakneck speeds. Sometimes the animals use one another for public transport, an effect that I have always found both touching and funny. Actually, these oxpeckers are feeding as they take a ride across the Mara in a lovely late-afternoon light.

400mm lens

I focused upon an individual in this mass of zebras that I encountered milling about in a clearing in Meru. I wanted the abstract patterns of many zebras with one ray of focused animal attention aimed straight out at the camera. That is what makes the picture work—that one alert animal intelligence beaming out of zebra patterns.

600mm lens

123

180mm lens

The bongo is an elusive animal rarely seen in the wild. Those that survive now live mostly in the thick forests on the slopes of the Aberdares. They have a genius for concealment. This one lives in captivity in the wildlife preserve of the Mount Kenya Safari Club.

600mm lens

I shot this image high up on a ridge in the Nairobi Game Park not far from Kenya's capital city. I was fascinated by the dust and the mood of the African landscape, which still has a feeling of animal abundance, primal remoteness, and a self-sufficiency in which humans are an alien intrusion. It is a mysteriously complete world, or seems so, even if it now must be enclosed and protected from the encroaching civilization just outside.

300mm lens

# BIRDS

They belong to a different order of wildness. It takes a little while to focus on them, as they seem at first to flit on the margins of the main four-legged, earthbound drama. Some photographers have begun to specialize in birds, finding them in some ways a greater challenge than animals. This red-billed hornbill, for example, fires through the African story like bright-feathered punctuation. The ostrich, of course, great feather duster of the plains, gets the prize for originality.

132 **I** photographed this hammerkop beside a stream in Masai Mara. The flowing textures of water and feathers made an interesting effect.

600mm lens

The ostrich is another of those African whimsies of design, as original in its way as the elephant or the giraffe. The ostrich is easier to photograph than the tawny eagle, which I usually spotted riding the high-altitude thermals. This alert bird had come to roost briefly beside a track in Meru.

600mm lens

135

**I** found this tea party of ostriches on a dry, barren stretch of Samburu late one afternoon. As I was used to seeing only one or two ostriches at a time, rarely more, I followed this group for half an hour, remembering what happened when I first encountered ostriches in Kenya in 1984 while doing part of an Olympics essay for *Time* magazine. As I photographed two Kenyan runners crossing a field near some giraffes, my camera bag lay nearby on the ground. While I was busy with my camera, an ostrich strolled up and swallowed two rolls of film. I turned in time to see the outlines of the film canisters descending the bird's long neck.

135mm lens

# CATS

They are the beautiful kings of the food chain: terrific sprinters, all speed and teeth and surprise. The Swahili word is *kali*—fierce. Their domestic side is more charming—their indolence and playfulness, the qualities that they exhibit when well fed.

141

600mm lens

In a lush Aberdares meadow, we came upon a pride of four lions. My safari guide said he had not seen lions there in years. One lion decided to check out the vehicle, and he stalked it as if it were his prey. That was unusual. As a rule, the animals on the game reserves are accustomed to cars and more or less ignore them. For very sound reasons, it is against the law to get out of a vehicle on the reserves: a lion seeing a person on foot would take a much more predatory attitude.

300mm lens

Everything is a matter of vantage. The cheetah spends much of its waking life scouting for its prey. I peer through the lens, having found mine. The cheetah, being the fastest animal on earth over relatively short distances, must make fairly fine calculations about the animals it hopes to run down. If the quarry has a decent head start, the cheetah will pull up panting and hungry at the end of its sprint.

800mm lens

143

Adult male lions, when not hunting, are among the laziest characters on earth, stretched out for endless hours in a heavy stupor. They have nothing to fear, of course, so almost nothing will rouse them except eventual hunger. Females, being closer to the young, have a friskier domestic life. This one in Masai Mara looked like any mother trying to restore order at a birthday party.

147

600mm lens

148

**M**ore than any other animal, perhaps, the lion carries his biography around on his face—his record of victories and defeats. When I spotted this male taking the thin shade of a thornbush in Samburu, I saw that his record of wins and losses was about even. Every lion is different. One has a scar, another has a chewed-up ear. One might look especially regal, almost as if his mane had been combed. Another is mangy and dusty and unkempt. I pulled my vehicle as close as I could to this prize-fighter, about 50 feet away, but he was indifferent to my work. To him, I was just part of my vehicle, a hard-skinned, prehistoric-looking beast of no nutritional value and emitting an ugly smell from the tail pipe.

600mm lens

I had been in Kenya for almost six weeks and had not yet seen a kill. It is all sheer luck. But on this afternoon in the Mara, I came upon a cheetah that had just run down a wildebeest. The victim was still alive. The pictures on this and the following pages show something of the matter-of-fact harshness always evident among the animals. Nature, of course, is not a sentimentalist.

600mm lens

155

180mm lens

157

400mm lens

T he animals have a way of striking splendid, almost stagy poses. In Amboseli I came upon a group of young cheetahs, probably a year old. I followed them for two hours, keeping a distance of 150 feet or so. Then one of them climbed this tree to reconnoiter the surrounding grassy plains to see if dinner was on the horizon.

(left) 300mm lens
(right) 800mm lens

**G**etting this picture (a favorite of mine) required two of the most important elements of animal photography, anticipation and patience. During their long hours of leisure, lions are sometimes playful, sometimes surprisingly tender with one another, like tabbies on the sofa of a New York apartment. I came upon these lions in Samburu. At first they lay in their midday torpor. Then one of them felt an affectionate impulse, and I photographed the result.

300mm lens

This picture was taken on an especially long and very rewarding day as my Land Cruiser was speeding back to camp. The sun had set 20 minutes earlier, and the light was fading fast. Out of the car window I spotted this lion, perched in an acacia tree, silhouetted against the darkening sky. I had the driver stop the vehicle. We backed up. With every lens I had, I shot away at the lion, who sat there as patiently as a fashion model, because with each lens, I bracketed my exposures. With silhouettes you can't be sure exactly which exposure will look the best.

180mm lens

# HOW IT IS DONE

BY NEIL LEIFER

164

SO YOU'RE LUCKY ENOUGH to be going on safari and want to know what to bring in the way of cameras, lenses, filters, film, and other necessities. Hunting with a camera—and that is exactly what you are going to be doing—is like no other photographic experience. You are in for the most wonderful, memorable time of your life. The two photo safaris that I have made were, without question, the most exciting experiences I have ever had.

ALL OF YOUR picture taking is going to be done from a vehicle, usually a Range Rover with an open roof. The game parks strictly forbid you to leave your vehicle. This serves one purpose: to make your safari totally safe, with no danger whatsoever. While your photographs of elephants apparently about to overrun you or lions stalking you, ready to pounce, may imply a different story, the truth is that while you are in your vehicle, you are in far less danger than you would be walking to your neighborhood grocery store.

A TYPICAL DAY will have you in your vehicle for about eight or nine hours (four in the morning, four or five at the end of the day). Because trails are very bumpy and the terrain extremely dusty, you'll need to exercise constant vigilance over your lenses and cameras. The vibrations of the ride cause screws to loosen and eventually fall out of your equipment. Bring along a small tool kit with jeweler's screwdrivers. Take the time after each excursion to be sure all the screws are tight and to check for any other problems. As for the dust, try to keep everything covered when not in use and bring a lot of lens tissue.

BOTH FROM a standpoint of enjoying yourself as well as getting great pictures, the simpler you keep things, the better. Two camera bodies should be sufficient, but a third would be a nice bonus. Today's 200mm lenses are fast and sharp enough so that you can get away with two zoom lenses and two long telephoto lenses. My choices for the zooms are a 35mm–70mm lens and a 80mm–200mm lens. The 80mm–200mm is particularly useful in many situations. As for the telephoto lenses, I recommend a 300mm and, if possible, a 400mm. You may need to use a unipod with these longer lenses, although many of the new lighter lenses are quite small and can be hand held if your shutter speed is 1/250 of a second or faster. A 2x times tele-extender will turn your 300mm lens into a 600mm and your 400mm lens into a 800mm, for those few times when you need to get that close. A unipod is recommended if you shoot with the tele-extender. Tripods are unnecessary and, in any case, there won't be space to use them in your vehicle. The only other lens you

might consider is a superwide angle, such as a 24mm or 28mm lens. I also recommend polarizing filters, which can come in handy on those occasions when the clouds and sky are brilliant.

THAT'S IT for the equipment. It may seem like a lot, but everything I suggest will fit into two shoulder camera bags. As for light meters, I recommend using the through-the-camera meters, since the light is quite tricky. The air in Africa is very clean and clear, and you are often at elevations in excess of 6,000 feet. Therefore, read the meter carefully. It usually knows more than you do.

LAST BUT not least, film! Since you want to bring a lot of film, I recommend that you use only one type and don't mix and match. My favorite is Kodachrome 200, which will work well in almost all of the lighting situations you will encounter. For the serious amateur, bring some slower film, such as Kodachrome 64. In a perfect world, I would divide my film supply equally between Kodachrome 64 and Kodachrome 200.

THE ONLY other suggestions I've got are to have a great time and plan a big party when you get home. The pictures you show your friends will do more for the safari business than any office of tourism.

# INDEX